100 OF THE BEST CURSES + INSULTS IN ITALIAN

Mille grazie to Elena Columbi and Vincenzo De Salvo
(my Italian language consultants, who so nobly double-crossed their own
motherland in the name of empowering her opposition forces), Chuck Gonzales
(whose illustrations made this book much funnier than it really is), and Jeannine Dillon
(the hippest, edgiest, funniest, and most supportive editor around).

Illustrations by Chuck Gonzales

Skyhorse Publishing books may be purchased in bulk at special discounts for sales promotion,
corporate gifts, fund-raising, or educational purposes. Special editions can also be created to specifications.
For details, contact the Special Sales Department, Skyhorse Publishing, 307 West 36th Street, 11th Floor,
New York, NY 10018 or info@skyhorsepublishing.com.

Skyhorse® and Skyhorse Publishing® are registered trademarks of Skyhorse Publishing, Inc.®,
a Delaware corporation.

Visit our website at www.skyhorsepublishing.com.

10 9 8 7 6 5 4 3 2 1

Library of Congress Cataloging-in-Publication data is available on file.
ISBN: 978-1616-08739-5

Printed and bound in China by South China Printing Co. Ltd

100 OF THE BEST CURSES + INSULTS IN ITALIAN

by Kirsten Hall, illustrations by Chuck Gonzales

LEARN HOW TO GIVE 'EM HELL LIKE A NATIVE!

I must preface this book by saying: I heart Italy. I'd even go so far as to say it's my first true *amore*. I've traveled to many other remarkable places, but Italy and I, you see, we've had a love affair for almost 20 years. In fact, now that I think about it, my actual romance with Italy is pretty much gone, our relationship remaining profound but in a more platonic way. Sort of like the couple that has lived together so long that things like bad breath no longer matter. Italy and I, we're now old friends.

Once a year, I return to it, like an overused cell phone in need of a good charge. If I were to create my own romantic fresco depicting what I adore most about Italy, it would include the world's finest shoes, pasta, wine, art, *gelato*, architecture, and (I'm married now, so I'll include this last "element" with a nod to the past) men.

And though my fresco would not include the following, it's not to say they don't exist in Italy (and in fact, sometimes in abundance—especially in certain regions!): aggressive beggars, pickpockets, snobs, hotheads, mobsters, bullies, ingrates, slobs, liars, vultures, and perverts. Yes, they're there. Italy may very well be superior to the rest of the world in most ways, but is indeed just like the rest of us in others in that it is resplendent in its own vermin as well as beauty.

And so it is in response to the latter group, the people who might try to intercept your love affair with Italy, that I equip you with the following hundred-plus insults. Fight back. Be brave. And it's quite likely you'll discover Italy as your lover, too. Just as long as you don't forget, those are my sloppy seconds!

PRONOUNCING ITALIAN

Spelling and pronouncing Italian are easy once you know the few basic rules. The chart below should help give you a feel for the rhythm of the language:

ITALIAN	SOUNDS LIKE	EXAMPLE	PRONUNCIATION
au	ow	*autobus*	ow-tobus
ce	che	*cena*	chayna
ci	chee	*cibo*	cheebo
che*	kay	*barche*	barkay
chi*	kee	*chiave*	kee-avay
ge	jay	*gelato*	jay-lato
gi	jee	*gita*	jeeta
ghe*	gay	*traghetto*	tra-get-to
ghi*	gee	*ghiaccio*	geeat-cho
gli	lyee	*degli*	del-yee
gn	ny	*ragno*	ranyo
iu	yoo	*aiuto*	a-yooto
sc (e/i)	sh	*scena*	shayna
sch*	sk	*schermo*	skermo

*c and g are hard except when followed by "e" or "i" — to make them hard in Italian an "h" is added.

Double letters **"ss," "tt," "ll, "**etc. are distinctly pronounced — with a slight pause between the two: **posso** pos-so, **gatto** gat-to, **pelle** pel-lay.

Stress usually falls on the next-to-last syllable. We have indicated the stressed syllable with bold in the pronunciation of the phrases.

SITUATION #1: OFF THE HOOK

Never satisfied with the way you experienced Rome as a hostel-hopping pseudo-hippy twenty-something, you've come back to collect. You check yourself into a lavishly-appointed landmark hotel with unobstructed views of the Spanish Steps and Trevi Fountain. Your spanking new suede Ferragamo loafers (the love children of at least five grade-A swine hides) are loving your feet in a way your ex-girlfriend never quite managed. Giving your favorite filmmaker (Fellini) the nod, you sidle up to Harry's Bar and order yourself a bellini. Your living "*la dolce vita*" (the sweet life) vibe is received loud and clear by the hottest *modella* (model) in the room. You send her a drink. She returns with a wink. Just as you start to suggest slipping off to a quiet place where you can get to know one another, she whispers into your ear that her "companionship" will run you 500 euros. To top it off, your nosy asshole of a bartender makes a less-than-feeble attempt at concealing his snickers.

What to do:
Remind yourself that you're still the same rock star you were five minutes earlier. The only one poised to lose here is the tender, whose tip was just reduced to zilch (though he might not know it yet). So with your head held high (and comfort taken in the knowledge that your Pratesi hotel bed linens will remain pristinely disease-free), lean toward the bartender and smile conspiratorially as you boast:

What to say:

CHE MINCHIA GUARDI? ANCHE A ROCCO SIFFREDI OGNI TANTO LE COSE VANNO MALE!

"What the hell are you looking at? Even Rocco Siffredi fails sometimes!"

The bartender will understand your full meaning here since Rocco Siffredi is a hugely famous Italian porn star.

It's appropriate to say this because...

You are a stud! And it's not your fault you're found irresistible even by society's "harder-working" ladies.

In the know:

Don't take home a hooker unless you're prepared to find yourself behind bars of an altogether different kind! Before 1959, prostitution was fully legal in Italy and occurred primarily inside of *case chiuse* ("closed houses"). Then the *legge Merlin* (Merlin law) forced the closure of the *case chiuse*, displacing many prostitutes onto the streets. Today, understanding Italian laws as they pertain to prostitution can be just as challenging as pairing the right pasta and sauce: while prostitution is not actually a crime in Italy, "aiding, abetting, and, exploiting" prostitutes is!

Most of the prostitutes in Italy are students. The next largest population group? Housewives! *Arrivederci*, Windex!

EXTRA CREDIT

A few words you may want to know should you unwittingly find yourself engaged in a conversation with a hooker:

SEI SICURA CHE IL TUO PAPPONE SIA D'ACCORDO CON TUTTO QUESTO?

"Now you're sure your pimp is okay with this?"

LO CONFESSO: SONO ANCORA VERGINE.

"I must confess: I'm still a virgin."

ERI SERIA QUANDO DICEVI DI AMARMI?

"Did you really mean it when you said you loved me?"

SITUATION #2: LIKE A VIRGIN

You've been a Madonna fan ever since you were a little girl—and not the Madonna with the He-Man arms and accent thicker than last night's Ragu. The religous kind! So a visit to Florence's Uffizi Museum is your dream come true. At first, you're only slightly miffed by the young, local, hand-holding couple that keeps positioning themselves between you and each painting you've stopped to admire. Then, the handholding turns to petting (you breathe in and out slowly and deeply just like your yoga teacher taught you), which turns to tonguing (your ujai breath is becoming less and less effective), which turns to moaning (all concentration is gone, and you let out an exasperated sigh). By the time their tongue tournament is well into overtime, you realize you can't keep your own mouth closed any longer either.

What to do:
Loudly clear your throat. If that doesn't work, position yourself between Team Tonsil Hockey and whatever masterpiece they're blocking. Then step backward, "accidentally" knocking into the pair. If they still haven't come up for air, show them you actually command enough of their language to defend yourself!

What to say:

POSSO UNIRMI A VOI?

"Can I join in?"

or

PRENDETEVI UNA STANZA!

"Get a room!"

It's appropriate to say this because...

Proper museum etiquette (no food, drink, loud noise, or artwork c**ck-blocking) is what ensures that all patrons are afforded the opportunity to enjoy a meaningful experience at the cultural institutions of their choosing.

In the know:

Museum-going tourists who've "been there, done that" in Italy (having exhausted the Uffizi, the Academia, the Vatican, and all of the other major museums) may want to check out the more kitschy Pasta Museum (in Rome), the Gas Station Museum (in Milan), the Knowing and Playing with Waste Museum (in Torino), the Umbrella and Parasol Museum (in Piedmont), or the Climbing Boot Museum (in Treviso)!

EXTRA CREDIT

Some cultures are more prone to PDA than others. And in Italy, public displays of affection are rampant. As such, you may want to tuck away a few more admonishments:

1. *FATE PURE COME SE NON CI FOSSI!*

"No really, don't mind me!"

2. *NON VI SI STANCA MAI LA LINGUA?*

"Aren't your tongues tired yet?"

3. *SE VI LECCATE ANCORA UN PO' RESTATE INCOLLATI!*

"If you make out any longer you'll find yourselves stuck together!"

SITUATION #3: FENDI FAKE-OUT

Against your better judgment, you find yourself salivating over the Fendi handbags peddled by the very same Venetian *"vu cumprà"* (street vendor) that your hotel concierge cautioned you about. One particularly aggressive "salesman" insists (in well-rehearsed English) that his wares were made in the same exact factories as the real thing, from the same materials, based on the same designs, and using the same techniques. Your Catholic half reminds you that buying counterfeit goods is illegal and you could be hit with a "fine for fakes" of up to 10,000 euros if the police conduct a sweep and catch you with a knock-off. But your "Sunday-morning-is-for-sleeping-in" half simply can't help herself, especially after watching a hip local purchase the same model you've been eyeing for a mere 50 euros. When you go to pay for one yourself, the peddler feigns confusion—suddenly insisting that the bag costs double.

What to do:

Act as if you are reconsidering the purchase and hover nearby until he nets his next victim. Then, once the transaction is about to go down, introduce doubt into the new sucker's mind by sighing and saying:

QUELLO STRONZO MI HA IMBROGLIATO!

"That bastard cheated me!"

What to say:

The slimy sales guy wants you to cough up a hundred euros for a purse that, to tell you the truth, is a piece of crap. Say to him:

SENTI, NON CREDERE DI FOTTERMI
SOLO PERCHÉ NON SONO ITALIANO!

"Listen, don't think you can f**ck with me just because I'm not Italian!"

It's appropriate to say this because...

The same way friends don't let friends drive drunk, customers don't let customers get screwed.

In the know:

In the past decade, Italian police have majorly cracked down on counterfeiters of designer goods in the name of protecting its fashion industry. In fact, in August of 2005, a Philippine woman living in Florence was fined more than 3,000 euros for buying fake sunglasses!

EXTRA CREDIT

Now that you're speaking in Italian, try thinking in Italian, too! Here's how your thought process might go if you had actually forked over the hundred euros:

La borsa era tarocca.

"The bag was a fake."

Ma che cazzo!

"What the f**ck?"

Vuole svuotarmi le tasche!

"He wants to empty my pockets!"

SITUATION #4: BUY, BUY BABY

After a 3,000-calorie dinner-and-drink session with your *amici* (friends), you decide to stroll back to your hotel instead of sharing a taxi with the others. En route you are stopped by a feeble woman in a flowery skirt with a back hunched 85 degrees more than it should be at her age. Cradling a pilly blanket in her arms, she moans pitifully while inching her way toward you. "*Bambino, bambino*, my baby, my baby…" She extends an open-palmed and filthy hand toward your bleeding heart.

What to do:

Put away the tissues, you sentimental fool! There is no starving baby inside that filthy rag. When was the last time you heard a hungry baby keep so quiet, anyway? You've just fallen victim to one of the most common yet ingenious ploys used on tourists in Italy. So don't get sappy, get mad!

What to say:

LEVATI DAI PIEDI!

"Get lost!"

It's appropriate to say this because...

You work for your money. You don't beg or steal, even though the prospect often sounds significantly more appealing than your 9 to 5 misery. Remember that by giving a an aggressive beggar money, you're perpetuating the cycle. Help society by teaching those importunate slackers that bumming doesn't pay!

EXTRA CREDIT

Beggars can be persistent. It may take a couple of rebuffs to make your point. As such, here are some other useful phrases:

NON HO UNA LIRA, CAPITO?

"I've got no money, dig?"
Even though euros have replaced lira in Italy, Italians still understand and use this expression regularly.

LASCIAMI IN PACE!

"Leave me alone!"

And if all else fails, here's your silver bullet:

CHIAMO LA POLIZIA!

"I'm going to call the police!"

SITUATION #5: WAITER HATER

As luck would have it, an important client has taken you to dinner at a Florentine *trattoria* where the snooty staff doesn't speak a lick of English. Desperate not to reveal yourself to your gourmand colleague as the inexperienced and finicky eater you really are, you seize the moment when he slips away to the WC (bathroom) to beg communication with your waiter. Your attempt at miming a person twirling long noodles around a fork is met with a blank stare. So you sketch a mounding plate of noodles and meatballs on a paper napkin and hand it over hopefully. The next thing you know, your waiter has doubled over with laughter just as your client returns with puzzlement to the table.

What to do:
Dignifying the situation with as little fanfare as you can, turn to face your waiter with a smile as sweet as *vin santo* (a dessert wine from Tuscany) and deliver the following threat in the same tone you might use if introduced to the Pope.

What to say:

SE NON LA PIANTI DI ROMPERMI TI RIDUCO IN POLPETTE!

"Leave me alone or I'll make hamburger meat out of you!"

It's appropriate to say this because...
Unlike elsewhere in the world, where aspiring actors and model wannabes wait tables in order to scrape by and make rent, the service industry in Italy is one that is taken quite seriously. That said, just because your waiter is capable of memorizing who ordered the fried zucchini flowers, doesn't give him the right to treat you like an uncultured buffoon.

In the know:

While tipping is customary in some European countries, it is not expected in Italy. And don't let yourself feel guilty about that fact. You're probably being charged without realizing it for that the carb-o-licious basket of bread!

SITUATION #6: OH, MAN!

It's *amore* (love)—and it's official. After months of negotiation, your Italian stallion boyfriend has finally moved in with you! You can practically hear the wedding bells and *bambino* (baby) coos. You note with pleasure that said *ragazzo* (boy) seems to have settled into your space almost seamlessly before discovering with horror the following morning that he has claimed one of your three closet shelves for his 19—yes, that's correct, NINETEEN!—man-bags. When you ask him why a man—really anyone—should need so many bags, he counters that different bags look *bello* (beautiful) with different outfits. He may as well have just bagged your entire sex life, you're so turned off.

What to do:

Suggest he reconsider and get rid of at least half of his purses. If he refuses, ask him if he might need a shelf in the bathroom for his make-up, too. If that still doesn't work, redirect your approach and draw attention to his shrinking manhood.

What to say:

DICI CHE POTREBBE STARCI ANCHE UNA POMPA PER ALLUNGARE IL PENE SULLA MENSOLA?

"Think we can fit a penis pump on that shelf, too?"

It's appropriate to say this because...

This is the guy you're supposed to be spending your nights with. The one you're supposed to be sleeping with...as in more than just sleeping. And he has 19 purses? Your southern half is insisting that you sort out this metrosexual mess pronto.

In the know:

Italian men are truly comfortable with their own sexuality. They use terms of endearment for one another such as *bellissimo* (beautiful) and *caro* (dear) with enough ease that you may never feel 100% confident which team any man is really playing for. Things like hugging and kissing each other, staring at themselves in mirrors for long periods of time, and sipping on pink "girly" drinks are in no way indications of any man's sexual preference.

EXTRA CREDIT

Keep your "man" in check every once in a while with one of these reminders:

VOGLIO UN UOMO CON LE PALLE.

"I like my men with balls."

E' PER QUESTO CHE HO UNA RAGAZZA

"That's what I have girlfriends for."

SÌ, QUELLA GONNA TI FA IL CULONE

"Yes, your butt does look big in that skirt."

SITUATION #7: MAMMA MIA

In the beginning, you didn't really mind "taking care" of your Italian boyfriend. Little things—like bringing him five Peronis during extra time in a *futbol* match—didn't bother you one bit. Then you somehow got stuck doing his laundry when his not-so-white tighty-whiteys began creeping their way into your hamper. But now that he's got you ironing his work clothes, it's not just his shirts that are feeling heated. To make matters worse, he just casually informed you that his mother does a better job with the iron than you. *Oh no he didn't!*

What to do:

Leave the iron on top of the shirt just until it burns a nice crisp hole in the chest (but not long enough to actually start a fire). You need to show that mamma's boy just how skilled you really are with hot tools. Then tell him...

What to say:

VAFFANCULO A TE—E A TUA MADRE!

"Go f**ck yourself—and your mother!"

It's appropriate to say this because...

They both deserve to be cursed since you're not sure who is the guiltier of the two. While he's an ingrate, his mother is probably the reason why. Furthermore, insulting an Italian man's mamma is comparable to vandalizing his Vespa. If you're looking for a way to hit your "man" where it hurts, always aim for Mommy.

In the know:

More adult males live in their parents' home in Italy than in any other industrialized country. In fact, an international women's group called Stop Mothering Men (SMM) was organized with the specific purpose of forcing men to finally grow up!

EXTRA CREDIT

The next time your boyfriend compares you to his mother, you may want to counter with:

COSA PENSEREBBE MAMMINA?

"But what would Mommy think?"

TUA MADRE È UNA PUTTANA.

"Your mother's a whore."

FATTI STIRARE QUESTO!

"Have your mother iron this!"

SITUATION #8: PUBLIC ENEMY #1

You're late to meet some friends at a café, and you just can't figure out which *piazza* you're standing in (why do they all have to look the same, anyway?). While unfolding your unwieldy street map, you accidentally bump into a pervert sitting on some steps ogling a group of teenage girls by the fountain. And so the gesticulation war begins…after muttering something you're pretty sure wasn't very nice, he rolls his eyes at you in disgust. You shrug your shoulders in apology. He shakes his head. You thumb your nose. He flicks you the bird. And you blank. The only remaining option you can think of is to moon him—and that definitely ain't happening after all of yesterday's *zeppoles*! You really want to be the bigger person, because deep down you know who you're dealing with here—some lonely loser who should be spending his time in anger management classes, not sitting in public places being pervy. But you can't help yourself. Your friends will just have to wait.

What to do:
It may take a few minutes—even hours!—but eventually some unfortunate soul will attempt to take a seat near *Signor Degenerate* on the steps. In a volume loud enough for all who are nearby to hear, issue the following warning:

What to say:

NON SI SIEDE MAI NESSUNO VICINO A LUI.
È FAMOSO PER LE SUE BOMBE.

"No one ever wants to sit next to him. He's famous for his loud farts."

It's appropriate to say this because…
While you don't actually know anything at all about this man's gas-passing habits, there's no question that he is environmental pollution in his own right.

In the know:

Many piazzas post signs detailing what is considered "polite comportment." Be prepared to be fined up to 40 euros for trying to go shirts-off in certain historic cities. You'll see lots of younger people doing it, but lying down on streets is also prohibited. Picnic lunches are also forbidden outside of parks. And don't even think about dipping your feet into fountains or canals!

EXTRA CREDIT

It's admittedly not a highbrow sport, but farting is kind of funny. In the right crowd (i.e., people with the maturity levels of teenagers), these flatulence-related phrases might earn you a few giggles:

HAI SCOREGGIATO?

"Hey, did you fart?"

CHE PUZZA!

"That stinks!"

ODORA LA MIA BOMBA!

"Smell my fart!"

SITUATION #9: LICENSE TO DRIVE

Your travel buddy suggests you forgo renting a car as planned to take you from Florence to Fiesole and hire a taxi instead. You're more than happy to oblige. After shopping and museum-hopping for five straight days, it's not only your fiscal resources that are spent. So while it will be a bit of a splurge, a "chauffeured" escape from the city into the hillside sounds like a justifiable one in its decadence. Your fantasy is shattered the second you cram your non-Italian (and thus too long) legs into the backseat of the matchbox-sized Fiat summoned by your concierge. And it's a safe bet that this driver's last name is Andretti. It's all you can do to keep down your blood orange juice as he bullies his way into chaotic multi-lane merges, disregards any and all lights and stop signs, and turns your relaxing drive into something that feels more akin to a sick game of "Chicken." The last straw is when he moves into the passing lane to pass a car that is *already passing another car*. You see your life flash before your eyes and are relieved that you have lit as many cathedral candles as you have, since that's probably the only reason you're still alive.

What to say:

MA CHI TI HA DATO LA PATENTE, SCEMUNITO?!

"Where did you get your driver's license, idiot?!"

It's appropriate to say this because...

That asshole almost cost you your life! End of story. And while it would have been appropriate for you to say something a whole lot more obnoxious, you're not too jetlagged to realize that your life momentarily remains in the f**cker's hands.

In the know:

Don't expect a taxi driver to stop for you anywhere but at a taxi stand in Italy. Taxi drivers are required by law to pay any injuries caused when they stop on the street—hardly affordable on their *piccolo* (small) salaries! So if you do try to hail a cab somewhere random, expect passing drivers to look at you, nod their heads, and cruise right on by.

EXTRA CREDIT

Not every taxi driver is honest when it comes to charging tourists. If you sense you're being cheated by a driver, one of these phrases might prove useful:

STAI SCHERZANDO, VERO?

"You're kidding, right?"

PERCHÉ COSÌ TANTO?

"Why so much?"

È DIECI VOLTE IL PREZZO SUL TACHIMETRO!

"That's ten times more than what is on the meter!"

SITUATION #10: GET A ROOM!

You probably should have known it was too good to be true. A room at a five-star Venetian hotel (on its own private island and accessible only by private water taxi) for about the same price as the mildewed motel you were stuck at for your cousin's wedding in rural Indiana last month seems like a no-brainer. Hell, you're going for the deluxe room instead of the standard for only an extra twenty euros a night! But when you arrive to check in, you're informed there aren't any rooms under your name. And, not that you could afford the non-special rates, anyway, but the hotel is completely sold out, to boot. To add insult to your jet-lagged injury, your desperate pleas for assistance are met with an unsympathetic stare by the cold-as-spumoni concierge.

What to do:
Beg your case once more. Maybe even insinuate a few pitiful circumstances that didn't necessarily happen but might make him slightly more compassionate (like someone stole your grandmother's only set of rosary beads out of your pocket at the airport). And if he's still staring at you with the same indifference, demand of him:

What to say:

CHE COSA CI FAI LÌ, FERMO COME UN BACCALÀ?
"What are you doing standing there like an idiot?"

It's appropriate to say this because...
A concierge, by definition, is someone who is "employed to make arrangements or run errands." And while a latte sure would be nice right now, you're not asking anyone to run errands. You're merely asking for help with your arrangement, which is, in fact, the service for which this jackass has been employed.

In the know:

The word "concierge" is derived from the Latin word *conservus* ("fellow slave"), and it means "keeper of the keys." Most European concierges are male, though men and women from around the world belong to Les Clefs d'Or, a professional concierge association with over 3,000 members in more than 50 countries. You can tell members by the gold keys they wear on their lapels.

EXTRA CREDIT

Concierges field their fair share of complaints. Here's how you can tell your Italian concierge you're dissatisfied at check-in:

LA MIA CAMERA FA SCHIFO.

"My room really sucks."

C'È TROPPO RUMORE.

"There's too much noise"""

VOGLIO UN RIMBORSO, TESTA DI CAZZO!

"I want a refund, d**ckhead!"

SITUATION #11: STRIKING OUT

While you'll reluctantly admit that Italy is superior to home in most ways (the food, the wine, the clothes—fine, if you really must concede, even the culture!), you still miss home and are ready to get back to the world as you know it. You've somehow managed to sit with enough weight (all right, it was disappointingly easy) on top of your suitcase (which is practically bursting at the seams with new leather jackets, designer shoes, and bottles of limoncello), and zip it closed. Check-out was a breeze (yay, tv check-outs!), and you arrive at the airport with the requisite two hours to spare. Parked at an airport café with a panini in hand, you notice with dismay on the departure screen overhead that your flight's been cancelled. The agent at your gate mutters something in broken English about another airline strike (the 17th of the week!) causing the cancellation. You ask what your options are from here, and she stifles a yawn while staring blankly back at you.

What to say:

MA CI FAI O CI SEI?

"Are you playing dumb—or are you really that dumb?"

It's appropriate to say this because...

Just because Italian airport is to strike as Easter is to chocolate doesn't make your predicament any more acceptable.

In the know:

Italian airlines and trains are infamous for going on strike. As such, always remember to check (ask your concierge to call or search online) to be sure your flight is on schedule before wasting time and money traveling to the airport only to find out you've got to turn right back around.

EXTRA CREDIT

Expect to have at least one logistical nightmare when flying in or out of Italy. A few choice phrases you may wish to unleash on airline workers who give you attitude include:

TI CONCI SEMPRE COSÌ PER LAVORARE?

"Do you always wear your finest clothes to work?"

COSA NE DICI SE RITARDO TUA MADRE?

"How about if I delay with your mother?"

TE LO DO IO UN BUON MOTIVO PER SCIOPERARE!

"I'll give you reason to strike!"

SITUATION #12: I SCREAM, YOU SCREAM

They say you are what you eat, and you're starting to see proof. Getting dressed after a week-long pasta-thon, and your legs have started looking creepily cannelloni-like. The only way you can think of to cheer up your deflated ego? Why, a *gelato*, of course. You arrive at your favorite *gelateria* with moments to spare before closing time. Unable to decide between the supremely dark *cioccolato fondente*, the heavenly and hazelnutty *nocciola*, or the egg custard-ee-licious *crema*, you order a scoop of each. Strolling back to your hotel, *cono* (cone) in hand, you take consolation lick #1 and feel your spirits instantly begin to lift. As you round a corner, a text-messaging teen knocks into your arm, sending your lifeline crashing to the ground. You watch with horror as the lout scurries onward, not even bothering to toss an insincere "*scusi*" your way.

What to do:

What not to do is much more obvious than what to do in this instance. No matter how heartsick you feel, don't convince yourself that no one's looking so you can get down on those hands and knees to collect—by hands or otherwise—that pool of liquid gold.

What to say:

TORNA QUI, BRUTTO STRONZO!

"Get back here, you ugly pr**ck!"

It's appropriate to say this because...

Your favorite *gelateria* may very well have closed for the night. But it's safe to assume that somewhere in the land of carbs you can still get yourself a thousand-calorie frozen replacement. And that little sh**t better be prepared to lead the way!

In the know:

One major difference between *gelato* and ice cream is that the former is churned much more slowly than the latter. The result is less whipped air, making for a denser, softer product. *Gelato* is also significantly lower in butterfat than ice cream. Another point for Italy!

EXTRA CREDIT

Bypass the tried-and-true basic *gelato* flavors for something unique instead!

CANNELLA	***MALAGA***
(Cinnamon)	(Raisin moscato)
CASTAGNA	***RISO***
(Chestnut)	(Rice pudding)
FICHI	***ZUPPA INGLESE***
(Fig)	(English trifle)
LIQUIRIZIA	
(Licorice)	

SITUATION #13: ROOM DISSERVICE

After a day spent in Milan's quandrangle fashion district, you finally understand the literal meaning of "shop 'til you drop." Back at your hotel, you kick off your Zanotti zebra peep-toe pumps and order an *antipasto* plate and a bottle of Montepulciano to be delivered to your room. 15 minutes later there's a knock on your door, and you hobble to answer it. The pimply room service delivery boy gives you a quick appraisal before suggesting something you're certain you've misunderstood. It sounds an awful lot like he's offering you more meat than what's on the tray. You ask him to repeat himself only to confirm that you heard his proposition loud and clear the first time.

What to do:

Grab the tray, point to the door, and tell the jerk-off to beat it somewhere else. Then pour yourself a nice big glass to help numb away that icky feeling.

What to say:

VATTENE, PICCOLO PERVERTITO!

"Get lost, you prepubescent pervert!"

It's appropriate to say this because...

This is definitely not what you expected when you chose this hotel based on its promise to deliver a "personal touch!"

In the know:

Montepulciano is a medieval town located in southern Tuscany. Montepulciano wine is rich with dark berry flavors and slight black pepper undertones. Don't be a show-off when serving it by giving it time to breathe. Unless it's an aged Nobile, the already-mellow wine doesn't need it.

EXTRA CREDIT

Below are a few items you may want to order in for room service. And don't worry, the concierge might make fun of you afterward, but the good news is you won't understand what he's saying anyway!

UNA CASSA DI BIRRA
"A case of light beer"

DELLA ROBA
"An 8-ball"

UNO SPOGLIARELLO
"A striptease"

SITUATION #14: OUT OF ORDER

You may not know how to speak much Italian—but, hey, you're not an idiot, either! The fact that *primo* means "first course" and *secondo* means "second course" isn't exactly rocket science. Still, you can't help the fact that you don't like the sound of any of the meat courses listed on tonight's menu. And you do want to try two of the pasta dishes. So you don't see what the problem is when you try to order an *insalata* followed by two *primi* instead of following the customary order of things on Planet *Ristorante Italiano*. Your waiter regards you with enough indignation, that if you didn't know better, you'd think you had just spit in his face!

What to do:

Repeat your order, perhaps more slowly and clearly, but definitely more firmly. It appears that a certain ball-buster needs a little reminding which of you is the paying customer! And if that doesn't work...

What to say:

FORSE TI SEI DIMENTICATO CHI È CHE PAGA, STRONZETTO?

"Perhaps you've forgotten who is paying whom here, you asshole?"

It's appropriate to say this because...

That Berlusconian bully needs a food chain reality check.

In the know:

Italian meals are generally served in the following order:

1) **ANTIPASTI** (appetizers, such as prosciutto and olives)

2) **PRIMI PIATTI** (first course, such as soup and pasta)

3) **SECONDI PIATTI** (entrée, such as meat or fish) with *insalate* (salad)

4) **DOLCI** (desserts)

EXTRA CREDIT

Serve up one of these three chewings-out to waiters in need of attitude adjustments!

SENTI UN PÒ: SEI UNO STRONZO

"Here's my tip: you're a jerk."

ORA CAPISCO PERCHÈ NON C'È MAI UN CANE QUI.

"Now I understand why this place is always empty."

ASSAGGIA QUESTO!

"Bite this!"

SITUATION #15: TRACK ATTACK

Ironically enough, you're off to Genoa (the birthplace of Christopher Columbus) for a day trip when you find yourself up against a logistical travel nightmare. The train *stazione* (station), teeming with heroin-pumped teens and enough cigarette smoke to give you second-degree lung cancer upon entry, is a typical Italian boiling pot of confusion. You have one hour before your train is scheduled for departure, and you spend 55 of those minutes in line waiting to buy a ticket from a testy window clerk. At last, ticket in hand, you head for the track number given to you by your *biglietteria* (ticket office) only to find a Naples-bound train waiting for departure. You run back to the antique information board where numbers and letters flip at a dizzying pace. You have two minutes remaining and are relieved when a respectable-looking man in uniform gestures to the train three tracks away. You barely make it up the steps (you'll worry about the ticket validation fee later!) as the doors close and the train begins to roll. You made it. That is, if you consider a day trip to Bologna making it. Because, with sinking heart, you are about to discover—yep, it's just as you feared—that bastard in a uniform lied to you. You're on the wrong train.

What to do:

Quicker than you inhaled last night's tiramisu dessert, scan the train car. Is there a window open even a crack? If so, you can still find satisfaction in the situation by yelling back at that sh**thead:

What to say:

QUALE TRA I TANTI UOMINI DI QUELLA PUTTANA DI TUA MADRE TI HA DATO IL SENSO DELL'ORIENTAMENTO?

"Which of your whore mother's boyfriends gave you
your sense of direction?"

It's appropriate to say this because...

You shouldn't need to be reminded why this is an appropriate thing to say—for occasions like this, when nothing but the big guns will do, your target is always Mamma!

In the know:

Getting on the wrong train by accident isn't the only kind of stinky experience you might find yourself in when traveling by rail in Italy. Worry less about restroom accommodations when traveling on larger, faster trains; they generally have plenty of bathrooms that are often surprisingly clean. For local trips, you might be better off waiting until you get to the next *stazione* —where you may have to pay, but it will be worth it!

EXTRA CREDIT

When assholes give you the wrong directions, give it right back to them!

DIVERTENTE, SEMBRANO LE STESSE INDICAZIONI PER LA CAMERA DI TUA MADRE.

"Funny, those sound like the same directions your mother gave me to her bedroom."

USI ANCORA IL TUO CAZZO COME BUSSOLA, EH?

"Using your d**ck as a compass again, eh?"

SITUATION #16: MISSING THE BOAT

You've been planning this evening for over a year, and now it's finally here. You're in Venice with the love of your life, a 2-carat ring in your pocket, and a question just begging to be popped. As you stroll *mano nella mano* (hand in hand) beneath a starry sky toward the surprise gondola that awaits you beneath the Rialto Bridge, the only thing that might possibly make this moment more perfect would be Pavarotti resonating through the air. Suddenly you feel the gondola tickets you've been holding in your other hand torn from your fingers, and the shadowy outline of a street kid fading into the distance.

What to do:
You can try to run after the punk, but the odds of catching him are as grim as the canal water. Street kids are speedy little buggers. You may as well kiss those tickets *arrivederci* (good bye).

What to say:

AVRAI BISOGNO DI UN CHIRURGO DOPO CHE TI AVRÒ RIDOTTO IN MILLE PEZZI!

"If I ever see you again, you'll need a surgeon to put your pieces back together again!"

It's appropriate to say this because...

That runt didn't just steal your gondola tickets. He stole one of the most precious moments of your life!

In the know:

It is said that there were thousands of gondolas in the 18th century. Today, there are only several hundred. A few are owned privately but most cater to tourists. The left side of a gondola is longer than the right side to help keep the boat from turning left at the forward stroke.

EXTRA CREDIT

Some gondoliers expect larger tips when they sing for their customers. Should you get stuck with an *American Idol* wannabe for a gondolier, you might want to ask him:

HA QUALCOSA PER IL MAL DI TESTA?
"Excuse me, sir. Do you happen to have any headache medicine?"

E PENSARE CHE UNA VOLTA QUELLA CANZONE MI PIACEVA!
"Can you believe I actually once liked that song?"

SENTITO RUMORE DI VETRI ROTTI IN LONTANANZA PER CASO?
"Did anyone hear glass just shatter in the distance?"

SITUATION #17: HELL, NO!

For the first time since that crop of bud hit your college campus ten years earlier, you feel truly blessed. Out of 12,000 people who have come to meet the Pope after Easter Sunday mass, you're #1,352 in line to kiss his ring. Five hours of tic-tac-popping and lip-licking later, you're #167 in the *baciamano* (kiss on the hand) line. And it's only a matter of another 45 minutes before you're on the Holy Father's deck. As you step toward His Holiness, he flashes you a broad smile while extending his right hand. You drop to your knees—and are suddenly blinded by a flock of *paparazzi* that has descended out of nowhere, cutting you off at the Pontiff pass.

What to do:

Wait! Don't do anything just yet. Think long—and think hard. You're as close to your Maker at this very moment as you'll ever be (especially if you do wind up putting your afterlife on the line by using one of the expletives listed below). That said, if you're relatively certain you'll be heading south postmortem, anyway (a safe bet if you've followed this book's instructions on even one occasion), you might as well tell those photographers exactly where they can go!

What to say:

VAI AL DIAVOLO!
"Go to hell!"

It's appropriate to say this because...
Those photo-hogs deserve the kiss of death after thwarting your one and only chance for salvation!

In the know:
Ancient Romans had different names for different kisses:
BASIUM: a kiss on the lips
OSCULUM: a kiss on the cheek
SAVOLIUM: a deep kiss

EXTRA CREDIT

And as for the assholes in the crowd who don't speak Italian, now you can tell them to go to hell, too!

GO TO HELL!

1. **ODI U KURAC!** (Croatian)
2. **VAL DOOD!** (Dutch)
3. **BRULER EN ENFER!** (French)
4. **FAHR ZUR HÖLLE!** (German)
5. **DRA TIL HELVETE!** (Norwegian)
6. **IDZ DO DIABLA!** (Polish)
7. **DU-TE LA DRACU!** (Romanian)
8. **IT AL INFIERNO!** (Spanish)
9. **GA AT HELVETE!** (Swedish)

SITUATION #18: WALK OF SHAME

You already know the definition of "sensible shoe" in Italian: schlumpy. And under normal circumstances you wouldn't be caught dead in anything other than high-rise kicks no matter how ill-fitting. But you had bunion surgery two weeks ago and your doctor insisted you wear "comfortable" shoes for at least a month. And now you're stuck doing the Reebok walk of shame through a Gucci shop filled with sneering saleswomen whose daily commissions make your annual salary look as measly as your self-esteem. One particular saleswhore (who still manages to look daintier than you even in four foot heels) sends the others into peals of laughter by muttering something you don't even need to know Italian to understand just tore you into pieces.

What to do:
Stand tall, sister. Reeboks are for athletes. And this Cinderella scene is nothing more than a game. A game that you're about to win.

What to say:

SPOSTATEVI DA QUI, INUTILI COMMESSE SNOB!

"Get over yourselves, you snobby worthless saleswomen!"

And as for the beeotch who made the snarky comment, just remember there's a reason her stick figure is working retail and not the runway:

FACCIA DI CULO!

"Butt ugly person!"

It's appropriate to say this because...

Bullying is a shield. Being condescending is how people cope with feeling vulnerable. With that in mind, don't let those offensive plays keep you down. Send your offenders straight where they belong—into the defense zone!

In the know:

When shopping in Italy, thick skin is as essential as your credit cards. Walk into a designer shop and prepare to be judged. From the color of your socks to the elastic in your hair, every little detail will be scrutinized—and you will be treated accordingly.

EXTRA CREDIT

Try one of these burns on for size the next time a saleswoman attempts to make you feel small.

PENSAVO SAPESTE CHE LE RIGHE ORIZZONTALI VANNO EVITATE.

"I'd think you of all people would know to avoid horizontal stripes."

PER FORTUNA ABBIAMO GUSTI DIFFERENTI.

"Luckily we have different tastes."

FORSE SARESTI PIÙ COMODA CON QUALCOSA DI MORBIDO IN VITA?

"Maybe you'd be more comfortable in an elastic waist?"

SITUATION #19: THE PRADA PUT-DOWN

When you carry it, you actually feel like a million bucks. And, appropriately, since it's hands-down the most expensive accessory you've ever owned: your Prada handbag. Sultry, sexy, and elegant—hell, it's a metallic masterpiece! And best of all, it's the real deal. That's right. It may have cost more than two month's rent for this authentic and ironically-dubbed "hobo" tote, but it was worth every missed-electricity-bill-payment penny. Because for the first time since the days of long ago when you actually fit into your size six jeans, your self-esteem is in mint condition. But your smugness loses its luster when a street vendor calls out to you as you sashay by, offering to sell you a replica of the bag's matching wallet. You gesture that your handbag isn't a fake. He sizes you up and chortles. Did he just challenge you? Um, yes, it appears he did!

What to do:

This is a tough one. Distinguishing between real and fake handbags really isn't easy—which is why the hawking industry is able to remain in business in the first place. Unless you happen to have your purchase receipt handy, you may need to resort to using a profanity in your own defense.

What to say:

SCOMMETTO CHE ANCHE TUA MOGLIE FINGE, CON UNA FACCIA COME LA TUA!

"With a face like yours, I bet your wife fakes it too!"

It's appropriate to say this because...

Not only is this street scum obstructing foot traffic with his phony purse party, now he's got the nerve to patronize you!

In the know:

Prada was founded in 1913 by Mario Prada. But it was Mario's granddaughter, Miuccia, who turned the company into the million-dollar business it is today with her invention of the brand's signature nylon handbag.

EXTRA CREDIT

In the market for a few more parting shots?

VEDI DI SPARIRE PRIMA CHE TI CAMBI I CONNOTATI!

Literally: "You'd better disappear before I fake your face!"

Basically: "You'd better disappear before I hit you until you're unrecognizable!"

MA NON LO VEDI CHE QUESTA È VERA, BRUTTO DEFICIENTE?

"Don't you see that this is real, asshole?"

TI FACCIO SENTIRE IO LA QUALITÀ DELLA MIA PELLE PRADA MENTRE TI CI STROZZO!

"I'll make you feel the quality of my Prada while I strangle you with it!"

SITUATION #20: McHATIN' IT

Your much-delayed flight gets you into the city late, and you're ravenous upon arrival at the hotel. You rule out room service upon the revolting discovery that the hotel restaurant's signature dish is tripe— a definite no-go. Just the idea of eating the lining of a cow's stomach makes you vomit a little in your mouth! And as far as you can tell from the crudely-translated and pretentiously-limited menu, the tripe is only the tip of the unappetizing iceberg. You pay a visit to the concierge and confess that you are a less-than-adventurous eater. With that, you offer him 20 euros for a tip on a local restaurant with more "pedestrian" fare. He smiles slyly and draws you a map while slipping your tip into his pocket. Two lefts, a street-cross, and a right turn later— and you're standing in front of a McDonald's.

What to do:

Just go in and order already, you hypoglycemic mess, you. The rest of the city has probably shut down for the night and you can't just assume that the concierge knew of other viable venue options for you at this late hour. That said, if you should happen to pass an open trattoria or two along your return route, you might become a little grizzlier about the whole deal…

What to say:

LA PROSSIMA VOLTA CHE MI PRENDI PER IL CULO L'UNICA RECEPTION CHE VEDRAI SARÀ QUELLA DELL'OSPEDALE!

"Next time you mislead me, the only reception you'll see
is the hospital one!"

It's appropriate to say this because...

You just paid 20 euros for that blockhead's two cents. And the worst part about it is that you could have easily McDined five times for that amount!

In the know:

Unlike other Mickey D locations, you might not be terribly disappointed by the ones in Italy. After all, a melted parmesan-topped burger on ciabbata bread sounds pretty damn civilized. So, *buon McAppetito!*

EXTRA CREDIT

Next time, tip that elitist bastard of a concierge with one of these epithets instead!

1. *STRONZO*
"Jerk"

2. *CAZZO*
"Pr**ck, D**ck"

3. *DEFICIENTE*
"Asshole"

SITUATION #21: FOUL PLAY

You remember reading in college that Sartre called Hell "other people." And after all of these years, you've finally had occasion to affirm his theory. Proof exists in the form of the space-invading jackass standing right next to you (no, make that pressing up against you like a canned sardine) on your bus ride to a Sardinian seafood market. To make matters worse, his breath smells like a week-old plate of *pasta alle vongole*.

What to do:
Procure a pack of gum from your purse and offer a piece to the offender. If he doesn't accept—and doesn't take at least one step back, either!—put that stink bomb in his place.

What to say:

CON UN ALITO COSÌ FETIDO CHISSÀ LE TUE SCORREGGE

"Your breath stinks so bad I bet people look forward to your farts!"

It's appropriate to say this because...
Hey, at least one of you needs to be fresh!

In the know:
In 1928, the Italian town Scrofano changed its name to Sacrofano. Why? Because the original name sounded much too like *scorfano*, the name of a brutally ugly fish!

EXTRA CREDIT

Why not be a little obnoxious yourself?!

IL TUO ALITO FA COSÌ SCHIFO CHE I DENTI SI NASCONDONO QUANDO PARLI!

"Your breath is so bad your teeth duck when you talk!"

IL TUO ALITO PUZZA COSÌ TANTO CHE IL TUO DENTISTA SI È SUICIDATO CON IL GAS

"Your breath is so bad that your dentist killed himself with gas!"

IL TUO ALITO PUZZA COSÌ TANTO CHE IL TUO MEDICO TI PRESCRIVE LE TIC TAC!

"Your breath is so bad you need prescription tic-tacs!"

CHIUDI QUELLA FOGNA!

"Shut your stinky mouth!"

SITUATION #22: TOUR DE FARCE

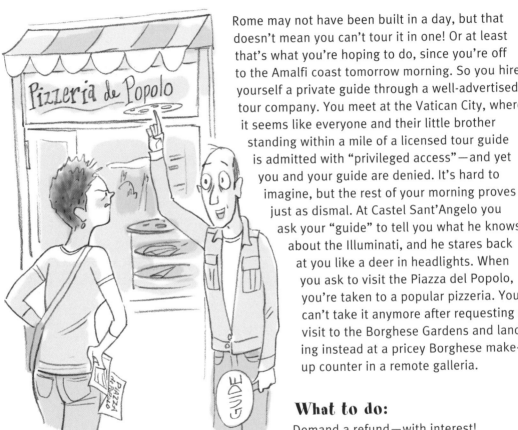

Rome may not have been built in a day, but that doesn't mean you can't tour it in one! Or at least that's what you're hoping to do, since you're off to the Amalfi coast tomorrow morning. So you hire yourself a private guide through a well-advertised tour company. You meet at the Vatican City, where it seems like everyone and their little brother standing within a mile of a licensed tour guide is admitted with "privileged access"—and yet you and your guide are denied. It's hard to imagine, but the rest of your morning proves just as dismal. At Castel Sant'Angelo you ask your "guide" to tell you what he knows about the Illuminati, and he stares back at you like a deer in headlights. When you ask to visit the Piazza del Popolo, you're taken to a popular pizzeria. You can't take it anymore after requesting a visit to the Borghese Gardens and landing instead at a pricey Borghese make-up counter in a remote galleria.

What to do:
Demand a refund—with interest!

What to say:

TI FACCIO FARE UN TOUR GUIDATO ALL'INFERNO SE NON MI RIDAI IMMEDIATAMENTE I MIEI SOLDI, ARTISTA DA QUATTRO SOLDI!

"I'll give you a guided tour to hell if you don't pay me back immediately, you con artist!"

It's appropriate to say this because...

This sham makes your grandma's decorative pillow collection look useful!

In the know:

By law, Italian tour guides must pass examinations given by local public tourist authorities and carry licenses. Unlicensed guides (i.e. taxi drivers) can chat with you all they want—but it's actually illegal for them to accompany you as your guide onto a site.

EXTRA CREDIT

Other words to make a phony tour guide feel like the worthless sh**t he is:

1. *VEDIAMO SE LA POLIZIA SA COME INDIRIZZARTI.*

"Maybe I'll see if the police know where to direct you."

2. *HO DEI DUBBI CHE TU NON VIVA SU QUESTO PIANETA.*

"My fist suspects you're in need of a little reality check."

3. *AVREI DOVUTO ASSUMERE TUA MADRE. ALMENO LA SUA TARIFFE SON MIGLIORI!*

"I should have hired your mother. At least her rates are better!"

SITUATION #23: ALL THE RAGE

Maybe the devil does wear Prada. It would make sense. After all, you've never seen anything as hot as what you're looking at in the window of Prada's European epicenter in Milan. And so, swinging open the boutique door with surprising ease, you are fully aware that you're about to trade in a year or two of future assisted living for something as frivolous as a wool-and-silk blend pantsuit (and telling yourself all the while, "Hey, the devil made me do it!"). You can practically hear your bank account sigh in relief when the pantsuit is too tight over your butt. And then when the sheer chiffon blouse makes you look too bust-tastic even for your boob-obsessed ex, you can practically hear HSBC saying "Uff!" (Italian for "Phew!"). The saleslady coldly suggests that you might be better off shopping elsewhere. After all, she explains, you and Prada aren't, how you say...a "good fit."

What to do:
Smile politely. Then find the shoe department. Do a quick inventory. Which pair will best deliver the kick in the ass that salesbitch needs? If you guessed the flower-stemmed heels, you'd be wrong. The python pumps? Well, now you're talking!

What to say:

ALMENO NON SONO COSÌ MAGRO DA USARE IL FILO INTERDENTALE AL POSTO DELLA CARTA IGENICA.

"At least I'm not so skinny I could use dental floss as toilet paper!"

It's appropriate to say this

because... Hell, if the shoe fits...

In the know:

Know your shoe size when shopping in Italian boutiques. They have a different measurement system in Europe.

Women	Men
5 – 6 = size $35\frac{1}{2}$	8 = size 41
6 – 7 = size $36\frac{1}{2}$	9 = size $42\frac{1}{2}$
7 – 8 = size $37\frac{1}{2}$	10 = $43\frac{1}{2}$
8 – 9 = size 39	11 = 45
9 – $9\frac{1}{2}$ = size 40	12 = $46\frac{1}{2}$

EXTRA CREDIT

Other insults worth feeding those anemic salesbitches:

1. *SEI COSÌ MAGRA CHE POTRESTI FARE L'HULA HOOP CON UN CHEERIO!*

"You're so skinny you could hula hoop with a Cheerio!"

2. *SEI COSÌ MAGRA CHE QUANDO PIOVE NON TI BAGNI*

"You're so skinny you could dodge raindrops!"

SITUATION #24: GOING WI-FRY

Ever since you were a lowly office assistant, you dreamed of the day you'd represent your company at the industry trade show in Bologna. Every coffee you brewed and delivered; every manuscript you copied and collated; every mundane task you completed with that perfectly practiced service-with-a-tooth-whitened-smile brought you one British Air mile closer. And now here you stand (or collapse, really, on top of your hotel bed—it's been a busy day at the fiera grounds). In the middle of typing up your day's notes, your laptop screen fades into darkness. Yup, out of charge. Rummaging through your suitcase you find the voltage adapter you bought especially for the trip. The one that the pimply salesgeek with the goatee at Radio Shack promised you would work. And the one that (of course) doesn't actually work. You place a call to the concierge who sends a "technician" (wait, isn't this the same guy who brought the extra toilet paper roll earlier?) to your room. After eying your computer, he rifles through a bucket of countless adapters and converters before finally grunting. You assume it's his indication that he found the one he was looking for. Jetlag trumps your instant distrust of this hotel "technician," and you plug the computer in. BZZZZ...BLEEP....ZOOM. Those are the final words of a laptop that has just fried to a crisp. In Italian, they might sound sort of like "*Ciao, ciao, ciao.*"

What to do:

Inhale deeply—but not so deeply that you take in any of the smoke.

What to say:

First things first. Express your frustration:

PORCO GIUDA!

Literally: "Judas pig!"
Basically: "Bloody hell!"

Then, calmly explain what you're going to do if the problem isn't remedied:

LA TUA FACCIA AVRÀ BISOGNO DI UN VIAGGIO AL NEGOZIO DI RIPARAZIONI SE NON MI AGGIUSTI TUTTO ENTRO UN'ORA!

"Your face is gonna need its own trip to the repair shop if you don't have this fixed within the hour!"

It's appropriate to say this because...

One hour of service really means ten hours to an Italian—and in ten hours, you'll be in your next meeting!

In the know:

Knowledge is power. So master a few of these key computer terms before talking to any more Italian techs!

Handheld: ***PALMARI***
Keyboard: ***TASTIERE***
Laptop: ***PORTATILE***
Memory: ***MEMORIA*** or ***RAM***
Monitor: ***SCHERMO*** or ***MONITOR***
Network: ***RETE***
Power supply: ***ALIMENTATORE***

EXTRA CREDIT

And if your machine still isn't fixed by morning? Upgrade your insults to:

1. ***SPERO NESSUNO TROVI I FILE CON LE FOTO DI TUA MADRE***

"Man, I hope no one finds the files with your mom's pictures."

2. ***GUARDA DOVE TI FICCO L'ADATTATORE TRA UN SECONDO...***

"See where I'm gonna shove the adaptor in a second...."

SITUATION #25: CUT THE FAT

It's your big birthday (the one you won't say out loud but that strongly resembles 40 with just a slightly larger first digit), and there's no pun intended about it. After celebrating with a Roman food fest for over a week, your clothes have started to feel more like sausage casings than apparel. At week's end, your husband surprises you with tickets to see *Aida* at the Teatro dell'Opera. Beneath a starry sky in the Baths of Caracalla, you feel like an ancient Roman princess. But the fantasy fizzles fast when the man behind you in the aisle at intermission confuses you for the opera singer. Okay, you knew you'd become pleasingly plump on this trip, but you haven't quite reached Madame Butterball status!

What to do:
Shattering some glass may sound good right about now. But try to stay calm and be the (ouch) bigger one.

What to say:

ABBASSA LA VOCE.
NON VORRAI CHE TUTTI SAPPIANO QUANTO SEI SCEMO!

"Keep your voice down.
You wouldn't want everyone here to realize what an asshole you are!"

Or, if you want to keep it simple, just call him:

CEFFO!

Literally: "Ugly face!"
Basically: "Jerk!" or "Asshole!"

It's appropriate to say this because...

You may be large, but you're also in charge!

In the know:

One theory as to why opera singers need to be large is that fatty tissue around the voice box increases a voice's resonance—and it's impossible to carry fatty tissue around the larynx without carrying it elsewhere, too. Sigh...

EXTRA CREDIT

And here's what to tell anyone else who wants to weigh in on your appearance:

1. **TUO MARITO NON HA DETTO CHE ERO GRASSA IERI SERA!**

"Your husband wasn't saying I was fat last night!"

2. **MOLTO BENE. TI SEI ACCORTO CHE SONO GRASSA. ORA DIMMI, QUANTE DITA STO ALZANDO ORA?**

"Very good. You noticed I'm heavy. Now tell me, how many fingers am I holding up?" (You know what finger to hold up here!)

SITUATION #26: SWEET REVENGE

Naples may be known for its rich history, art, cul- ture, and gastronomy—but for you it has only one association: limoncello. You can't seem to get enough of it—night after night after night (and, not that it's anyone's business, but some afternoons, too.) Yours seems almost like an abusive relationship, but without the extreme jealousy, emotional withholding, lack of intimacy, sexual coer- cion, infidelity, verbal abuse, threats, lies, broken promises, physical violence, power plays, or control games. Okay, wait just *un momento*. Suddenly your nightly affair with the sweet liqueur seems a whole lot healthier! So, it is with complete and utter delecta- tion that you accept your waiter's offer for an after-dinner limoncello on the house. The pours are as generous as the hottie who brings them to you, and four nightcaps later you've lost sight of your own night's cap. What could

you do? The waiter was a Leonardo DiCaprio look-alike! When the bill is brought to you in all of its blurry glory, you're about to sign it (hell, you'd sign away your firstborn at this point in the evening, you're so numb!) when a certain charge catches one of your cocked eyes. Four limoncellos at a thieving fifteen euros a pop?! Hey, weren't those supposed to be freebies?

What to do:

If puking comes easily, now might be a funny time to expel a little of that fury...especially if the tablecloth is made from high-quality linen!

What to say:

IL LIMONCELLO ERA FORTE, È VERO – MA NON COSÌ FORTE COME IL PUGNO CHE TI DARÒ SE NON FAI SPARIRE QUESTO SCONTRINO IMMEDIATAMENTE!

"That limoncello was strong, all right—but not as strong as my fist will feel if you don't adjust this bill immediately!"

Why it's okay to say it:

Because even with all of that sugary goodness coursing through your veins, you suddenly don't feel so very sweet.

In the know:

Limoncello is produced in Southern Italy from lemon rinds, alcohol, water, and sugar. It must be made with pure 96% alcohol and diluted only after extraction.

EXTRA CREDIT

And there's nothing like a schoolyard insult when you've had a few too many:

SARÒ UBRIACO, MA NON SCEMO!

"I may be drunk—but at least I'm not an idiot!"

SITUATION #27: DRIVER'S DREAD

In the age of the Internet, most things happen with so little effort that they seem almost automatic. To prove it, your day trip in Praiano just three hours earlier has already been added to your online blog and hit 21 times. And in under ten minutes, you've made a date with a *figa* ("hottie") you just met in an online chatroom. She lives in Ravello, a nerve-shattering 7km drive up the Valle del Dragone from Amalfi, but you have to admit she looks white-knuckle worthy. And so five minutes later you've secured yourself an online car reservation in just three easy steps. Enter name, click. Enter credit card info, click. Enter request for automatic car, click. *Finito*. When you arrive the next morning at the rental agency, you're informed that they only have stick-shifts (which you haven't driven since the time your girlfriend got too wasted to drive her own car in high school—and even then it was just down the block). The only difference between then and now is you know better than to think with your pants.

What to say:

ANCHE SE NON LO FARÒ, FAREI MEGLIO A PRENDERE COMUNQUE L'AUTO..MEGLIO RISCHIARE UN INCIDENTE STRADALE CHE DORMIRE ANCORA CON TUA MADRE!

"While I'm not going to do it, I probably should take the car—but only because I'd rather have an accident than sleep with your mother again!"

Why it's okay to say it:

While you could be sipping Amaltifinis witha 5-star babe in a town with world-class views, instead you've got this guy's ugly mug staring back at you.

In the know:

With a population of about 2,500, Ravello sits high in the hills above Amalfi. DH Lawrence and Virginia Woolf enjoyed spending time there, and Gore Vidal insists it has one of the most spectacular views in the world.

EXTRA CREDIT

Fuel up with these three additional insults:

1. *SE NON RIESCI A LEGGERE LA PRENOTAZIONE, ALMENO LEGGI IL LABIALE: C A M B I O   A U T O M A T I C O, TESTA DI MINCHIA!*

"If you can't read my booking, at least read my lips: A U T O M A T I C car, you asshole!"

2. *PRENDO LA MACCHINA IN CUI HA DORMITO TUA MADRE IERI NOTTE!*

"I'll take the car your mom slept in last night!"

3. *QUANTO SEI IGNORANTE DA UNO A DIECI?? CENTO!*

"How illiterate are you from one to ten? ONE HUNDRED!"

SITUATION #28: BUSTED!

You've done your homework. You know what to expect when it comes to Sicily— and you're not even a tiny bit scared. Purse snatchers, smurse schmatchers. Your new, concealed money belt is hard enough to find even without your increasing number of stomach folds. You practically double dog dare those petty thieves to try to tear your camera out of the ingenious bra-strap sling you boyfriend jerry-rigged for it (never mind the fact that you can hardly get it off your person yourself—which is actually kind of a bummer because it's going to cut back dramatically on your souvenir photo collection). Mob, schmob. You can recite every Don Corleone line from *The Godfather* in your sleep—what do you have to

be afraid of? And speaking of sleep, now that you've scored yourself the only seat left on the sleeper train that's about to take you there, you're ready to cut some serious z's. You sit back, close your eyes, and then *disgustoso*! Did someone just open your blouse and fondle your chest?

What to do:

Open those peepers and bust that peep-show pervert in action!

What to say:

QUANDO MIO PADRE AVRÀ FINITO CON VOI, IL PADRINO SARÀ VIETATO AI MINORI!

"When my father's finished with you,
The Godfather is going to look G-rated!"

Why it's okay to say it:
Because now — if for no other reason — everyone on the train can see where you've hidden your camera!

In the know:
Mafia families only began paying respect to their dons by kissing their rings after the release of *The Godfather*.

EXTRA CREDIT

Call a mobster or a mobster's wife one of these names and expect to find a horse head in YOUR bed!

BABBO:
"idiot"

CAFONE:
"boor"

IPOCRTIA:
"phony"

RITARDATO:
"dumb"

PUTTANA:
"whore"

SITUATION #29: BULL(Y)SH**T!

You've seen this face before. It's the same one that has haunted you since Kindergarten. That same moronic class bully who tormented you during your formative years—not because it made him any smarter, but simply because pantsing you in gym class somehow made him feel better about himself. And now he stands before you once again, this time reincarnated in the form of an Italian municipal registry office clerk. You quickly determine that you stand about as much of a chance at gleaning from him how to obtain an elective residence visa as you did getting your jock strap back in ninth grade. He keeps you waiting while he rearranges a paper clip collection on his desk. Then he spends another fifteen minutes grooming his unibrow in the reflection of a computer monitor. Finally, when he calls you up to his barricaded window, he befuddles you with rules that are as contradictory as seafood pasta and shaved asiago. You need to open an Italian bank account and transfer all of your money into it before you can get a visa, but most banks won't let you open an account without a visa. You must purchase a home before you can get a visa, but you can't purchase a home without a bank account which you can't get until you have a visa. You suddenly understand how this dimwit must have felt while taking the very same high school exams you aced with your eyes closed.

What to do:
When you can no longer take his ear-f**cking for another second, tell that ruffian what you've been dying to say to him since you were ten—but, even better, tell him in Italian!

What to say:

SEI LA PROVA VIVENTE CHE L'UOMO DI NEANDERTHAL ESISTE ANCORA!

"You're living proof that Neanderthals still walk the Earth!"

Why it's okay to say it:

It's about time you finally defended yourself. (And now go get some underpants that don't have Spider-Man on them and become a real man once and for all.)

In the know:

Becoming an Italian resident can be a bureaucratic nightmare. But acquiring a permission certificate as a "long-term visitor" is actually quite simple. Proving you have sufficient money to support yourself while staying is usually enough to get you one of these.

EXTRA CREDIT

Let the battle of the wits (or dimwits, as the case may be!) continue...

1. *TI INVITEREI AD UNA GARA D'INTELLIGENZA MA NON MI METTEREI MAI CONTRO UN AVVERSARIO DISARMATO!*

"I'd engage you in a battle of wits but I never fight an unarmed opponent!"

2. *TU, CARO MIO, SEI UN ARGOMENTO CONVINCENTE PRO ABORTO.*

"You, my friend, make a compelling argument for abortion."

3. *NO SCUSA, PRIMA DI ASSUMERVI QUA DENTRO FANNO UN TEST DI SUPIDITÀ?*

"Did you have a stupidity test before being hired in this place?"

SITUATION #30: PITY IN PINK

You've been waiting at the bar all night, and quite frankly you don't get it. You've got "I'm available, so go ahead and hit on me already, you effeminite, pink-drink-sipping, pathetic excuses for men!" written all over your Pupa concealer-coated face. And it doesn't hurt that your Dolce & Gabbana bustier dress is skimming your body just the right amount—enough to reveal your thrice-weekly Stairmaster routine but not quite enough to disclose your Spanx line. Asked objectively, you'd say you're looking good. No, not Isabella Rossellini good—but hotter than at least 90% of your competition. So when you finally get your first nibble, the real surprise is that it took as long as it did. Sure, he's wear-

ing a pair of skinny jeans that are so small you couldn't have even poured yourself into them back in the third grade. And he's not actually as tall as his 3-inch-high gelled hair might imply. But he's holding up two strawberry margaritas and, well, that's sort of sweet. Besides, enough tequila and anything is negotiable. You reach out to accept his offering, and he snorts "I am only dating *modelle*!" before pirouetting off into the crowd.

What to do:

Grab the closest cocktail from the bar and hurl it at that meglomaniacal *metrosessuale*.

What to say:

NON LO VOLEVO COMUNQUE IL TUO DRINK DA FEMMINUCCIA!

"I didn't want your girly drink anyway, you cream puff!"

Why it's okay to say it:

Because your only other alternative is a bitch slap—and you're pretty happy with your manicure.

In the know:

Don't assume that the pretty men in Italy are also stallions in the sack. In fact, a medical congress in Rome established that six out of 10 Italian women find their boyfriends and husbands to be dissatisfactory partners in bed!

EXTRA CREDIT

Skip the scratching, hair-pulling, and shirt-shredding. Try settling this catfight with words!

INTENDEVI DIRE MODELLI...
"You meant male models..."

C'È UNA DIFFERENZA DI PIÙ O MENO OTTO CENTIMETRI TRA NASCERE PERSONE NORMALI O DEGLI STRONZI.
"There is an 8cm difference between being normal and being an asshole."

SITUATION #31: HEAD'S UP!

Isn't it ironic? On one hand your wife is about to divorce you because she claims you don't communicate well enough, and on the other hand it's your communication skills that seem to be the problem. Between time spent on your home phone, cell phone, BlackBerry, desktop, laptop, and video chat station, you don't have a minute to toss her way. And so, even though you don't think there's enough Xanax in the world to get you through it, you've agreed to go on a getaway *sans electronics*. As she explains, you must rekindle (now don't get any ideas there, guy—your Kindle is off-limits, too!) your romance. It's all quite eerie at first. So much time to, well, think. Snuggling in the morning. Strolling in the afternoon. After-dinner promenades along winding canals and through the narrow cobblestone streets of Venice. For the first time in decades your head suddenly feels clear. And then wet. And then heavy. And then…fishy? You reach up to see what happened and a hunk of cooked fish flops out of your hair and onto the sidewalk, landing in a pool of vinegar, onions, and pine nuts. Someone just dumped their dinner scraps out the window and caught you in the crossfire. You've been dumped, all right—just not in the way you imagined!

What to do:
If you can reconstruct from which apartment the dish actually dropped, it might be worth grabbing a fillet and hurling it back through its window.

What to say:

PREGATE CHE NON VI TROVI, A MENO CHE NON VOGLIATE FARE DA ESCHE POVERI LECCACULO

"Don't let me catch you unless you want me to make bait of you, you lowly bottom-feeder!"

OR

66

CHE CAVOLO TI METTI A LANCIARE CIBO DALLA FINESTRA? SEI FUORI COME UN BALCONE, COSO

Literally: "What the hell are you throwing from the window?
You must be out as a balcony, dude."

Though the literal translation is "out as a balcony," it's like saying you're "out of your mind."

Why it's okay to say it:

Sardines may be brain food, but only a senseless idiot would toss leftover dinner out of his window. This is the 21st century!

In the know:

Sarde in Saor is a classic dish found in many of Venice's wine bars. Fresh sardines are bathed in wine, vinegar, and a touch of sugar and then topped with pine nuts and raisins. The dish is served at room temperature and is likely to swim its way into the hearts of even the sardine-skittish.

EXTRA CREDIT

Fight future nasty air raids with these even nastier words:

SCEMO!
"Idiot!"

STRONZO!
"Asshole!"

COGLIONE!
"Jerk!"

PEZZO DI MERDA!
"Piece of sh**t!"

SITUATION #32: CROSSING THE LINE

After being swindled out of 200 bucks on a bus ride through San Francisco last spring by two guys who just happened to have a deck of cards and who just happened to know a fun little game (which you later learned was Three Card Monte), you'd think you'd be a more cautious tourist. But no, not ever-gullible you. You're the type to trust every Tom, Dick, and Harry (or, as the case may be here, every Tommaso, Riccardo, and Enrico) you meet along your travels. And so, after searching unsuccessfully for the pre-purchased ticket holder line at the Sistine Chapel in Rome, you ask a cute *ragazzo* (boy) sitting with his buddies for directions. The line to which he directs you seems impossibly long, but you don't think to question it—even after one of them high-fives another for reasons you don't quite understand. So when you finally reach the front of the line an hour and a half later and are informed by a testy teller that you're in the wrong place and cannot proceed forward without buying an altogether new ticket, you're as pissed as yellow piazza steps.

What to do:

You could pretend you don't understand what you're hearing and proceed with indifference toward the entrance. But do bear in mind it's highly unlikely you'll get very far with all of those guards standing around, hungry for an activity other than their usual ball-scratching.

What to say:

D'ACCORDO, ALLORA. CREDO ANDRÒ A UNIRMI ALLA FILA DAVANTI ALLA CAMERA DI TUA SORELLA!

"Okay, then. I'll just go join the line outside your sister's bedroom!"

CULO DI SCIMMIA

"You look like a monkey's ass!"

It's appropriate to say this because...

Just like The Last Judgment, good must always triumph over evil.

In the know:

Besides being a heavenly destination for art enthusiasts around the world, the Sistine Chapel is where a new pope is elected by the College of Cardinals.

EXTRA CREDIT

Religious tourist attractions are the perfect spots for a little blasphemy:

1. *PORCO DIO!*

"Goddamn!"

2. *PER L'AMOR DI DIO!*

"For God's sake!"

SITUATION #33: ALL TAPPED OUT

You're not an idiot. You watch the nightly news (when there isn't a *Friends* re-run on, that is). And, as such, you're well aware that your beloved bottled water is actually no more than a cog in the carbon-belching industrial machine. But you simply can't help yourself. While others may insist that water is water is water, to you it's much more than a colorless, odorless, and tasteless substance. No thanks to that mug of crap from a tap! Yes sirree, spring water packaged in pretty aqua-tinted plastic is your vice of choice. So when you order a bottle of Lurisia to accompany your soup, you're appalled when the waiter brings you a glass of something cloudier than your *stracciatella* (Italian egg-drop soup) and insists it is Lurisia.

What to do:

Toss the contents of your glass at your waiter and then point out he shouldn't worry—spring water doesn't stain.

What to say:

NON SARÒ ITALIANO MA NEMMENO IDIOTA.
PORTAMI SUBITO QUELLO CHE HO ORDINATO, COGLIONE!

"I may not be Italian, but I'm not an idiot either.
So bring me what I ordered, you cheat!"

It's appropriate to say this because...

Unlike your water, you were totally clear about what you ordered.

In the know:

Lurisia water is collected from a spring located at the base of the Western Alps. The spring was discovered in 1917 at which time its water was analyzed and approved by Nobel Prize winner for physics and chemistry Madame Curie.

EXTRA CREDIT

Need a few more insults as dirty as your tap water?

1. *MA COS'È QUESTA ACQUA PUTRIDA, CRETINO!*
"What is this putrid water, idiot?"

2. *COMBINAMI UN'ALTRA CAZZATA E TI LINCIO!*
"If you f**ck things up again, I'll have you lynched!"

3. *SE QUESTA È LURISIA IO SONO LA MADONNA!*
"If this is Lurisia, then I'm Holy Mary!"

SITUATION #34: THE BREAKING POINT

In typical Italian fashion, the "laws" for navigating your way around a roundabout (traffic circle) are totally illogical (if not downright insane). What—you thought because you were driving there first that you actually had the right of way or something? Get real! Because while the purpose behind a roundabout may be to keep traffic flowing quickly and safely through busy junctions, what is about to happen is anything but safe. Turning along with the rest of the traffic, you realize you can't remember which exit you want. So, just to be on the safe side (ha!), you decide to take an extra lap. Cruising along in the inner lane (a strategic move made in an effort to avoid all on- and off-roundabout merging mania), your heart stops when—LOOK OUT!—a car so small it could be mistaken for a ziti noodle zooms into your space and then off into the distance up ahead, taking your side mirror along with it as a souvenir (and leaving behind nothing more than a cloud of smoke).

What to do:
Your testosterone is flaring, but resist the urge to chase after that devil-may-care speed demon if you still hope to make it out of that death trap in one piece.

What to say:
But if that American road rage kicks in and you simply can't control yourself, hit that pedal to the metal and tell that SOB:

GAREGGERÒ SUL TUO CADAVERE!

"I'll race you to your coffin!"

It's appropriate to say this because...

Hell, your car is bigger, and you've got insurance!

In the know:

Italy's drunk-driving laws are stricter than those in the U.S., only allowing 0.5 milligrams of alcohol per milliliter of blood. The U.S. limit is a little more generous at 0.8%, though this can vary from state to state.

EXTRA CREDIT

Still feeling road rage?

TI FARÒ MANGIARE LA MIA POLVERE!
"I'll let you eat my dust!"

MA AMMAZZATI!
"Go and kill yourself!"

DIETRO IL VOLANTE DI OGNI PICCOLA AUTO C'È UN PICCOLO STRONZO!
"Behind the wheel of every small car is a small pr**ck!"

SITUATION #35: THE TIP-OFF

Red flag #1: The taxi driver at Rome's Ciampino airport refuses an elderly Italian couple waiting in front of you in the line, insisting on escorting you into the city, instead. (Presumably because you're having such a good hair day.) Red flag #2: The ride to your hotel takes roughly four times as long as the hotel web site said it would. (There is a bit of unexpected traffic, albeit light.) Red flag #3: When you arrive at your hotel, it's suspiciously nowhere in sight and your driver gestures down the street, his arms insisting he cannot go the wrong way down a narrow one-way street. (Admittedly not an ideal situation for a nervous tourist visiting a city for the very first time, but you're not opposed to staying on the right side of the law, either.) At long last, when the driver hands you a receipt with a hand-written figure that differs greatly from the significantly smaller number on his meter, your own crap-detector meter finally sounds.

What to do:
Rifle through your wallet as if procuring your fare until your luggage has been unpacked and set on the curb. Then get out of the car and set that crook straight.

What to say:

SE PENSI CHE TI DIA ANCHE SOLO UN EURO DI QUELLO CHE MI HAI CHIESTO SEI PIÙ LOGORO DEI TUOI PNEUMATICI

"If you think I'm going to pay you even one euro,
you're about as sharp as your rubber tires!"

It's appropriate to say this because...

If he gives you a hard time, all you'd have to do is suggest you'd be happy to ask the *polizia* to help you the rest of the way!

In the know:

Taxi drivers looking to scam you are a dime a dozen. If you aren't too overloaded with luggage, consider taking a bus, train, or hotel shuttle instead. And if you simply must take a cab, be aware that many cities have ordinances mandating set fixed rates for rides between airports and city centers.

EXTRA CREDIT

Tip your driver with one of these pieces of advice!

1. *NON MI FOTTI, STRONZO!*
"Don't f**ck me, asshole!"

2. *SEI UN LADRO TRAVESTITO DA TASSISTA, ECCO COSA SEI.*
"You are a thief dressed up like a taxi driver, that's what you are."

3. *TI BUCO LE GOMME SE NON SPARISCI ALL'ISTANTE!*
"I'll cut your tire if you don't vanish right now!"

SITUATION #36: DINNER FOR ONE

Having worked the late shift in a diner for two years while putting yourself through grad school, you can usually spot an episode of dine-and-ditch from a mile away. So you're totally perplexed when you're the one who gets chewed and screwed (and not at all in the way you were hoping!) on your first date with the *bello* (cute guy) you met on today's train ride to Turin. At first you suspect he's still in the bathroom, perhaps suffering from a little *stomaco* upset. But when the restaurant-plaguing rose-peddler passes you by three times before returning with a special offer she reserves for solo dining patrons, you may as well stick a fork in yourself—you're done.

What to do:

Tell the snickering waitstaff whosestares suggest you're the most exotic thing they've seen since beef cheek ravioli...

What to say:

E IO CHE PENSAVO CHE LA TRIPPA FACESSE SCHIFO!

"And I thought tripe was ugly!"

It's appropriate to say this because...

You were already prepared to fake it tonight, anyway.

In the know:

Since 1678, when a royal decree authorized Turin's production of chocolate, it has become one of the chocolate capitals of the world. The *gianduiotto*, a celebrated sweet that dates back to the 19th century, is made from a coca-hazelnut paste. Also originating in the 1800s is the city's *bicerin*, a frothy hot chocolate and coffee blend.

EXTRA CREDIT

Skip the chew and say "screw you!" to those bottlenecking waiters.

CAGATI IN MANO E PRENDITI A SCHIAFFI!
"Sh**t in your hand, and then slap yourself in the face!"

POTEVA ALMENO PAGARE IL CONTO, QUEL MALEDUCATO!
"At least he could pay the bill, ill mannered!"

E TU CHE TE NE STAI LÌ IMPALATO A GUARDARE, PORTAMI LA CARTA DEI DOLCI!
"What the hell are you looking at? Bring me the dessert menu!"

SITUATION #37: DOWN AND DIRTY

Plagued by writer's block while attempting to complete the 500+ page mystery you've been working on for over three years, you flee to Venice to give your mind a break from the pressure of tying up so many loose knots. After three days of Chianti, *cicchetti*, and calm unlike anything you've known since before your wife gave birth to your twins, the plot suddenly reveals itself to you while you sip on your third *caffè corretto* at an outdoor café. You whip out your laptop and the keys begin to tap themselves. When you surface for air three hours later, your novel has an ending. And not just any ending, mind you—but a perfect one! You are literally skipping your way across the Rialto Bridge, back to your hotel to call your editor to share the good news, when, halfway across, a leather-clad ruffian snatches your notebook. No way, no how. You don't care what it takes to get that computer back. Even if it means falling into the murky canal water below, then that's just what will have to happen! And then three shoves, a hair pull, and a kick in the balls later, it does.

What to do:
Brush the algae off your face and hold up the computer in victory. He's not the only one who knows how to play dirty!

What to say:

PRONTO PER IL SECONDO ROUND, PERDENTE?

"Ready for round two, loser?"

It's appropriate to say this because...
Having marinated in murky Venetian canal water, you're truly ready for anything.

In the know:

Venetian canals are world-famous. Venice's roughly 150 canals are like watery streets. People get around Venice on foot, by gondola, or by *vaporetti* (motorized water buses); cars aren't allowed.

EXTRA CREDIT

Ready to get down and dirtier?

1. *QUESTO CANALE HA UN ODORE FAMILIARE. SARÀ MICA APPENA PASSATA TUA MADRE?*
"This canal smells familiar. Was your mother just here?"

2. *MANGIATI LA MIA MERDA BRUTTO BASTARDO!*
"Eat my sh**t, you bastard!"

SITUATION #38: UNDER THE TUSCAN RUN

Far outside of Florence lies the real Tuscany. The kind of Tuscany that Frances Mayes told you all about. The kind of place where the pitfalls of city living vanish into lavender-scented air. The Tuscan countryside is heaven in its purest essence, and if you happened to stumble upon a villa for sale along your day-long bike ride, you might even just surprise everyone responsible for your graying hair back at home by pulling your own Frances and buying it on the spot. You slow your *bicicletta* as you pass a bewitching villa hidden behind an ancient ivy shell. A weather-worn sign leans precariously against the front door's glass. You rub your eyes in disbelief after seeing your two favorite words in the Italian language: "*In vendita*" ("For sale"). The idea of living miles away from civilization leaves you feeling deliriously giddy, and you hurry back to your *bicicletta*, having committed the telephone number listed on the sign to memory. But your soaring heart sinks when you discover the dozens of sticks poking out of your bicycle spokes. What? When? And most importantly, who? And then the evidence. The mischievous giggles fade as the children escape.

What to do:

You don't have a choice here. Chase them. Their legs are likely half as long as yours, which means (in theory at the very least) that, since you can still hear them, you should be able to catch them. You knew all those hours laboring on the treadmill weren't for nothing!

What to say:

CHI VUOLE UN OCCHIO NERO?

"Which one of you is in the mood for a black eye?"

It's appropriate to say this because...

These little buggers may very well become your new neighbors. And, as such, you need to nip their pranks right in the lavender-scented buds.

EXTRA CREDIT

Sticks and stones won't break their bones, but they could elicit some tears!

1. *VI FACCIO RIDERE IO, APPENA VI BECCO!*

Literally: "I'll make you laugh as soon as I get you!"

Bascially: I'll be the only one laughing when I get you!

2. *FIGLIO DI PUTTANA!*

"Son of a bitch!"

SITUATION #39: JUST BEAT IT!

Malnourished models to your left. Depthless designers to your right. Arrogant actors to your front. And pernicious politicians to your rear (how very à propos!). You're in with the in crowd after somehow making it past the ball-busting bouncers blocking the doors of one of Milan's most famous *discotecas*. The music is thumping, the dancers are pumping. With just a sliver of light to lead your path, you make your way onto the dance floor just as the DJ breaks into a funky house set. But each move you bust is met with an unwanted grope or unappreciated grind. Less than a minute into the fondle-fest you simply can't stand the harassment anymore.

What to do:

Show the next pervert who lays a hand on you your latest and greatest dance move: the beat down!

What to say:

E QUESTO LO CHIAMI BALLARE? SEMBRANO LE MOSSE DOVUTE A UN'INFEZIONE INTIMA.

"Oh, that was a dance move?
I thought maybe you were moving like that because your STD was burning."

Or if your clever comeback will get lost in the chaos of the club, just yell (loud enough for all to hear):

VECCHIO SPORCACCIONE!"

"Dirty old man!"

It's appropriate to say this because...

Now you're not the only one to feel exposed!

In the know:

Not only is it illegal for men to grope you on the dance floor (it's true!), but a recent ruling from Italy's highest court makes it illegal for men to touch their own genitals in public, too!

EXTRA CREDIT

Meet sexual harassment with verbal harassment:
PUOI TOGLIERE PER FAVORE LA TUA MANO DA DENTRO LA MIA CAMICETTA?
"Could you please remove your hand from inside my blouse?"
PIÙ CHE IN DISCOTECA SEMBRA DI ESSERE IN UN BORDELLO.
"This looks more like a whorehouse than like a club."

SITUATION #40: TAKEN FOR A RIDE

It's late when you arrive at the *stazione*. So late, in fact, that even the teenage junkies who call the station home are too beat to beg (despite the fact that the logo that patterns your Coccinelle handbag might as well be a euro sign). And the only taxi driver in sight is too busy rolling himself a sloppy smoke to notice all 6 feet of your blonde self. The web site said your hotel was a close walk from the station. But even a short walk in your new Miu Miu kitten heel flex pumps seems an impossible feat. (Who named these things, anyway? Flex? Liars!) Your charm bracelet jingles as you hobble your way toward the sole taxi, rousing the driver from his sleep-smoking session. You fold up your legs in order to fit into the backseat of his matchbox cab and then dozens of left turns ensue. You guess it must be all of those Italian one-way streets you read about in your guidebook. Rome sure has a complicated road system! At long last, you arrive at your hotel, too tired to complain to hotel management about misrepresenting its proximity to the station. The next morning, when you take a right out the hotel door and practically walk straight into the station, you realize that last night you were taken for an even bigger ride than you had realized!

What to do:

Wait until evening and then return to the station. Odds are you'll find that moonlighter waiting for his next "job" in the very same spot.

What to say:

SPERO TI VENGA PIÙ FACILE ORIENTARTI IN PRIGIONE!

"Let's hope you have an easier time
finding your way around your prison cell!"

It's okay to say this because...

There are city ordinances designed to protect tourists from con-artist cabbies, and the law is very much on your side.

In the know:

If you think you've been ripped off by a cab driver, and he insists you pay, explain that you plan to call the *carabinieri* (police...the number is 112).

EXTRA CREDIT

Tell the next stick-up artist just where he can stick it!

1. *QUESTA VOLTA TE LO FACCIO FARE IO UN GIRO TURISTICO DELLA CITTÀ, A CALCI IN CULO PERÒ!*
"This time I'll give YOU a long tour of the city, by kicking your ass!"

2. *GRAZIE A CIALTRONI COME TE LA CITTÀ È IMPRATICABILE.*
"Thanks to scoundrels like you the city is impassable."

3. *SPERO SARAI PIÙ BRAVO QUANDO TI CONSEGNERAI ALLA POLIZIA!*
"Let's hope you do better getting yourself to the police station!"

SITUATION #41: BLACK AND BLUE

Game on! Your superstar of a concierge just scored you a ticket to one of the year's most highly-anticipated *futbol* matches. You know the fan rules: wear the same colors as your team. Italy (you remember, after seeing them play last year back at home) wears black. Lucky for you, the black t-shirt you packed for your trip to the Bahamas a few months earlier is still rolled up in a ball in the side pocket of your suitcase. Indeed it smells a little gamey—but that actually makes it seem all the more appropriate. Sitting in the stands, Peronis in both hands, you think you're seeing double when two burly, blue-clad men move in close on either side of you. What you are about to learn with a little help from their fists is that Italy wears black for away games—and blue for home. And for wearing a t-shirt in the opponents' color, you're about to wear both colors on your face.

What to do:
Nothing. You f**cked up. Don't hate the players. Hate the game.

What to say:

E' STATO UN ERRORE INNOCENTE, LO GIURO — SONO UN TIFOSO ITALIANO!

"It was an honest mistake. I swear—I'm an Italy fan!"

In the know:
The Italian national soccer team is called *Azzurri*, Italian for light blue. Italy won the 2006 World Cup final, before a television viewership of over 700 million people.

EXTRA CREDIT

If you're brave enough to rattle off a few curses while getting pummeled, then try some of these on for size:

1. *LASCIAMI STARE, BASTARDO!*
"Let me go, you bastard!"

2. *FOTTITI!*
"Go f**ck yourself!"

3. *INCASSA QUESTO, STRONZO*
"Take this, pr**ck!"

SITUATION #42: SPACE INVASION

The Galleria dell'Accademia isn't that big. Nor is Michelangelo's *David*, the museum's main attraction, you discover even from afar with bemusement. (Suddenly your ex seems more well-endowed than you remembered!) But what is big is the crowd. It's nearly impossible to actually get near David. And after forgetting your glasses and waiting in line outside for over two hours to see the statue "up close and personal," you'll just have to wait and push along with everyone else until you have the chance to get closer. Two steps forward. Push. Another step. Shove. Elbow. You make progress, albeit slowly. And then, at long last, the crowd parts and *David* is yours, in all his, ahem, glorious splendor. You begin to take him in when suddenly the pervy guy behind you presses into your backside with his own rock-hard "masterpiece."

What to do:

Let out a loud cough, summoning the attention of those around you. Then turn around and tell that jerk-off:

What to say:

E IO CHE PENSAVO CHE IL DAVID FOSSE PICCOLO!

"And I thought David was small!"

In the know:

The "crown jewels" on the cast of *David* displayed in the South Kensington Museum (now the Victoria and Albert Museum) were covered during visits from Queen Victoria and other prestigious women with a detachable fig leaf.

EXTRA CREDIT

Other insults for puny-peckered pervs:

1. *HO UNO ZIO CHE SAREBBE MOLTO CONTENTO DI CONOSCERTI...*
"I have an uncle who would be VERY happy to know you..."

2. *TI APPOGGERESTI PER FAVORE AL DIDIETRO DI QUALCUN'ALTRO, GRAZIE!*
"Could you please lean against somebody else's back, THANKS!"

3. *SAI DOVE TE LO PUOI FICCARE QUEL GROSSO PALO?*
"You know where you can put your big pole?"

SITUATION #43: BLEAT STREET

For most tourists, driving in Italy is difficult at best and terrifying at worst. But after a week of touring the country in your rental car, you've got the "laws" of the road down pat. Ignore all stop signs, speed signs, and traffic lanes, weave often, and pass (extra points on narrow roads) whenever possible. Essentially, anything goes. And as long as no one dies, it's all good (or "*vabbe!*" as the Italians would say). So as you rocket your way down the *autostrada* toward the airport (note to self: next time remember the time difference when arranging a hotel wake-up call!), you're shocked to discover there's still one remaining road rival for which you haven't prepared: the unforeseeable flock of sheep. *Baa! Screech! Crash!* When you recover from the crash shock, you instantly pick up a scent that you'd recognize anywhere after getting even with last year's materialistic cheat of an ex-girlfriend. Yup, the smell of expensive burning wool.

What to do:
You could bleat back, but you probably don't want to feel even crazier than you already do. So start working on finding the shepherd you intend to lambast, instead.

What to say:

ORA CHE SAPPIAMO CHE ODORE HA UNA PECORA BRUCIATA, CONFRONTIAMOLA CON L'ODORE DI UNA TESTA DI CAZZO ARROSTITA!

"Now that we know what burning sheep smell like,
let's compare it to the scent of a roasting asshole!"

In the know:

It is not uncommon for sheep grazing in fields to make their way close to (and sometimes even onto) roads. If you should find yourself in a fender bender with a flock, slow down and gently edge your way past it. Be especially careful when driving at night. Sheep often sleep by the side of the road — counting cars, perhaps!

EXTRA CREDIT

And here's what to tell your insurance agent since you probably don't have sheep-smashing coverage:

1. ***VORREI ENTRARE NEL TUO CERVELLO PER PROVARE LA SENSAZIONE DEL VUOTO ASSOLUTO.***

"I would like to be in your brain to feel the sensation of absolute emptiness."

2. ***AL POSTO DEL CERVELLO HAI UN CARTELLO CON SCRITTO "AFFITTASI".***

Basically: "You have a 'FOR RENT' sign where your brain should be."

3. ***CHE CIALTRONI TU E L'ASSICURAZIONE DA DUE SOLDI PER LA QUALE LAVORI!***

"You're both scoundrels, you and the insurance company you work for!"

SITUATION #44: HOLY CRAP!

According to the map, you're close. You can even hear the sweet sounds of a choir echoing faintly through the barren cobblestone streets. But once again, the same shoddy sense of direction that caused you to pass your own house three times in one day (when you were SOBER, to boot!) is giving you the old run-around. Suddenly you stumble upon (or rather, into) the only villager not in church service this Sunday morning. "*Scusi!*" ("Excuse me!") you ask the gentleman. "Where is the church?" And then you remember the word in Italian. "*Chiesa?*" you add, shrugging your shoulders and opening your hands at your side. The man smiles and nods, offering you his open palm. Clearly he didn't understand your question. You're not looking to make a new friend. So you try again. "*Chiesa?*" you ask, cupping one hand over your eyes like a visor and looking to the left and right. The man nods and offers you his opened hand once again. You don't understand.

"*Non capisco!*" ("No understand") you admit. "Two euros for directions," he deadpans in English.

What to do:

You'd love to crucify the thief, but remember you're moments away from entering one of God's temples!

What to say:

MA CHE CAZZO STAI DICENDO? PENTITI ORA SE VORRAI CHE DIO PERDONI IL TUO CULO SPIACENTE!

"What the hell are you talking about?
Repent if you want God to forgive your sorry ass!"

It's okay to say this because...

God may be slow to anger—but you're not!

In the know:

When visiting Italian churches, make sure your clothes cover both your knees and shoulders. Find out if the use of a camera is prohibited before taking photos. Don't eat or drink inside the church. And last but certainly not least, do not enter a cathedral while a service is in progress!

EXTRA CREDIT

A little more ammo for your holy war:

1. *BRUCIA ALL'INFERNO, MENDICANTE DA STRAPAZZO!*

"Burn in hell, you worthless beggar!"

2. *DUE EURO EH? VEDIAMO QUANTE MONETE DA DUE RIESCO AD INFILARTI NEL CULO!*

"Two euros? Let's see how many two coins I can insert in your ass!"

3. *SE TI PRENDO TI SPEZZO, PORCO GIUDA!*

"If I take you I'll break you, dirty Judas!"

SITUATION #45: URN BURN

As an elementary school teacher, you're not the type to attend high-ticket auctions (at least not on your current salary!). But you do understand how they work, especially after watching the Victoria Beckham-wannabe moms of your second-graders drown their 20-pound bodies in vodka tonics before paddling their way into bankruptcy in the name of "winning" the aquarium-themed class quilt. So when you attend a local art auction, you're delighted to discover it's not the cat-fight kind at all. Murano chandeliers, Byzantinian mosaics... each piece up for sale is more awesome than the next (or is it the Montepulciano goggles you're suddenly sporting?). Another glass and that blurry terracotta Etruscan vase up for bid looks like a steal at 1000 euros. You sip your wine and wave your paddle...once, twice, three times. At 3000 euros, your paddle is still mid-air when the auctioneer announces the winner and everyone claps. What, are you invisible or something? Is that even possible with crimson teeth?

What to do:
Throw your paddle at the auctioneer, but be careful not to hit the vase en route unless you're really able to pay for it (which, when you sober up you'll remember – you're not!).

What to say:

COSA, NON HAI VISTO LA MIA PALETTA? SEMBRA CHE SIA TU IL VERO PEZZO ALL'ASTA, POLITICO DISONESTO!

"What, you didn't see my paddle?
Looks like you're the real piece of work at this auction, you political phony!"

In the know:
The Etruscans lived in what is now known as Tuscany. No one knows for certain where they came from originally, but the characteristics of their artwork (which was clearly influenced by the Greeks) suggest they likely hailed from Asia Minor.

5 WAYS TO INSULT A GUY'S MANHOOD

ALLORA SEI COSTRETTO A SEDERTI ANCHE TU PER FARLA! A MENO CHE NON HAI A DISPOSIZIONE UN A PINZETTA!

"You need to sit to take a leak...unless you have a pair of tweezers with you!"

NON TI SALIREBBE NEMMENO SE SCARLETT JOHANSSON TI CHIEDESSE DI LECCARLA COME UN GELATO.

"You couldn't get an erection even if Scarlett Johansson asked you to lick her like an ice-cream."

VEDI DI RIUSCIRE ALMENO A INFILARLO PRIMA, FRETTOLOSO!

"At least try to put it in first, hasty!"

HAI IMPARATO A CAMMINARE SULLE MANI PER VEDERTELO DRITTO?

"You learned how to walk on your arms just so you can see yourself with a hard-on?"

MI PIACEREBBE FARE SESSO CON TE, SE SOLO LO TROVASSI...

"I really want to have sex with you, if only I could find it..."

5 INSULTS THAT COULD GET YOU LYNCHED

DIRTI FIGLIO DI PUTTANA SAREBBE OFFENSIVO PER LE PUTTANE!

"To call you a son of a bitch would be offensive to bitches!"

UNO STRONZO FUMANTE È PIÙ SEXY DI TE!

"A hot piece of sh**t would be sexier than you!"

CHE TI MUOIA LA FAMIGLIA IN UN INCIDENTE STRADALE.

"I wish your family dies in a car accident."

SEI UN FALLITO DEL CAZZO. INCAPACE, RITARDATO, SFIGATO!
NON VEDI CHE NON TI CAGA NESSUNO?

"You are a f**cking failure, a slow mind, a dork!
Don't you see that no one gives a sh**t about you?"

5 OF THE BEST "YOUR MOTHER" INSULTS

SE TUA MADRE CUCINA COME FA I POMPINI, SAI CHE PRANZI SQUISITI!

"If your mother cooks like she gives bl**wjobs, she'd make delicious lunches!"

TUA MADRE È TALMENTE RELIGIOSA CHE SE VEDE UNA
CAPPELLA DEVE PER FORZA INGINOCCHIARSI!

"Your mother is so religious that every time she sees a *cappella*, she has to kneel!"
(In Italian, a *cappella* is a part of the church AND a part of the male genitalia.)

TUA MADRE È TALMENTE STITICA CHE HA DAVVERO UN ALITO AGGHIACCIANTE!

"Your mother is so constipated that her breath is terrifying!"

TUA MADRE È COSÌ GRASSA CHE QUANDO SI FA LA DOCCIA I PIEDI NON SI BAGNANO.

"Your mother is so fat that her feet don't get wet in the shower!"

TUA MADRE È COSI BRUTTA CHE LE TENDE A CASA TUA LE HANNO
MONTATE I VICINI DA FUORI.

"Your mother is so ugly that neighbors came to install the curtains from outside."